WS

Weather around the world

"Where in the world" from Curriculum Visions

Mum and Dad,

...ng a wonderful time
...sunny Thailand.

...nda X

700027632710

D0314135

Dear Garry,

The sun is shining in Blackpool today but it was very different yesterday. It was cloudy and there were a few showers so we couldn't get down to the beach.

We're off to build a sandcastle. Bye for now.

Love, Liz

Dr Brian Knapp

Desert sunset

Curriculum Visions

Curriculum Visions is a registered trademark of
Atlantic Europe Publishing Company Ltd.

Atlantic Europe Publishing

First published in 2005 by
Atlantic Europe Publishing Company Ltd.
Copyright © 2005
Atlantic Europe Publishing Company Ltd.

Author
Brian Knapp, BSc, PhD

Art Director
Duncan McCrae, BSc

Editor
Gillian Gatehouse

Senior Designer
Adele Humphries, BA, PGCE

Designed and produced by
EARTHSCAPE EDITIONS

Illustrations by
David Woodroffe

Printed and bound in China by
WKT Company Ltd.

Weather around the world – *Curriculum Visions*
A CIP record for this book is
available from the British Library

Paperback ISBN 1 86214 480 X
Hardback ISBN 1 86214 482 6

Acknowledgements
The publishers would like to thank the following:
Alexander, Catherine, George, Justin and
Octavia Crowe.

Picture credits
All photographs are from the Earthscape Editions
photolibrary except the following: (c=centre t=top
b=bottom l=left r=right)

*Courtesy of the University of Dundee page 30br; NASA
page 26tl; NOAA page 25tl; ZEFA pages 21tr, 25tr.*

*This product is manufactured from sustainable managed
forests. For every tree cut down at least one more is planted.*

There's more on the Internet

Free information, pictures and details of our related
products can be found at:

www.CurriculumVisions.com

Contents

Hot air balloons move up into the sky much like the parcels of invisible air that will make clouds.

What will the weather be like?

We need to know what the weather will be like today, tomorrow, when we are on holiday and in the future.

A "Where in the world" postcard from Curriculum Visions

Dear Mum and Dad,

I am in a rainforest on the equator. It is hot and sticky every day. They tell me it is the same all year. Each day the weather is the same, too. It starts with a sunny morning, then the cloud gathers and by afternoon torrents of rain are falling. No wonder this is not a popular place for holidays.

Love Pushpa x

Let's go out tomorrow! Oh, wait a minute, what will the **WEATHER** be like?

Let's go on holiday to Florida! Oh, wait a minute, what will the weather be like there?

There are lots of things we like to do, but if they are outside, we always need to know what the weather will be like.

Actually, there are two kinds of weather we want to know about. We want to know what the weather is going to be like from day to day so we can plan what we are going to do in the next few hours. Also, we want to know what it will be like from **SEASON** to season across the world, so we can plan our holidays.

Weather worldwide

The world has many types of weather, and they are mostly not at all like ours. Some places are hotter, some colder, some wetter and some have no **RAIN** at all. Some are wet at one time of the year and dry the rest of the time.

▼ **If you were travelling to a tropical rainforest, this is what you might pack in your rucksack.**

A "Where in the world" postcard from Curriculum Visions

Dear Sis,

Aloha, as they say in sunny Hawaii.

It's hot and sunny here today. We haven't bothered to look at the weather forecast because it's the same great weather day after day. Funny, I thought the hottest and sunniest place would be the equator, but it turns out to be just half way there. It's just like being in Spain, but with surf. Well, I must be off to the beach.

Wayne

▼ If you were travelling to warm, sunny Hawaii, USA, this is what you might pack in your rucksack.

Travel bag

When you plan what to take on a holiday, what influences your choice? Probably the weather first of all. On these pages you will find some travel bags. Look at them and see how different they are. Each one is designed to be right for the holiday someone is taking.

Look at the contents of the rucksack on page 6, and see how it is packed with warm clothes for the cold snowy mountains. Then look at the choices for the tropical rainforest on page 4. This is a part of the world where it is hot, but it also rains a lot. Then look at the items packed for a visit to warm sunny Hawaii shown above. Finally, compare all of these with page 7 that shows what people might take on a holiday in the UK.

Suppose we go on holiday and we find it is cold and wet? That would ruin our holiday. Suppose we choose to go into town and find that, later in the day, it pours with rain and we don't have our waterproofs with us. That will ruin our day out.

For all of these reasons, we need to know about the weather where we are and the weather in other parts of the world, too.

Weather clues

One way you can get clues as to what to take with you is to look at pictures of that place and see what people are wearing. But be careful, these pictures are taken on nice days at the best time of year, which does not necessarily mean it is like that all of the time. For example, think how a collection of holiday pictures of British holiday resorts downloaded from the Internet only tell you about the sunny summer days. If you lived in Australia and imagined it was like this all year, and arrived in Britain in winter, you would be in for a big surprise!

▲ By knowing about the weather in the winter Alps, the cold, and the need to guard against sunburn even in winter, this is what you might pack in your rucksack.

A "Where in the world" postcard from Curriculum Visions

Dear Grandma and Grandpa,

This is a picture of where we ski. It's bitterly cold, but OK when the sun shines. It snows quite often, so the snow is very deep and the skiing great! There are lots of people here in the high parts of the Alps during the winter and they still have snow here even though it's March.

Lots of love,

Jessica

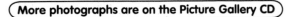

A "Where in the world"
postcard from Curriculum Visions

Dear Auntie Ada and Uncle Fred,

We are touring in Oxfordshire. Yesterday it rained, but today it is lovely and sunny. The weather forecast says it will stay nice for two days and then cloud over, so we plan to go to the seaside in Kent tomorrow and visit the funfair on the cloudy day.

Mandy and Marie

▼ To cope with the changeable British summer this is what you might take with you in your rucksack.

What this book will tell you

In this book we shall see why some places are hot, some cold, some wet and others dry and why some places have damaging **WINDS**. We shall also see how changes happen through the seasons. We shall also find out how to measure temperature, rain and wind. We shall also find out about weather forecasting and some kinds of weather that can produce disasters. Finally, we shall see why it is different in different parts of the world and why the world's weather may be set to change in the future.

Weather patterns around the world

The long-term weather varies a great deal across the world.

We think about the weather in two ways: the day to day changes, and what it is like on average. The map on this page shows you what it is like on average all over the world. This is the sort of information we need to know when planning our holidays.

Hot and cold places

The Earth heats up most around its middle, the region called the tropics. Here the Sun shines overhead every day. By contrast, it is much colder near the poles where the Sun rises to only a low angle in the sky. We live in the middle, a region called the **MID-LATITUDES**, and here it is mild, not hot or cold.

The world's weather bands are mainly caused by how warm or cool it is and they run roughly parallel with the equator.

Rainy and dry places

Rain mainly falls in places close to oceans where winds bring moist air onshore. Places like the UK, which gets lots of onshore winds, have wet weather. Places far from oceans or places where winds blow offshore have much drier weather. These are some of the reasons that weather is not divided into simple bands that run right around the globe.

▼ ① **This map shows the main types of average weather (CLIMATE) across the Earth. Notice how the climates are mainly laid out in bands parallel to the equator. Different amounts of rainfall and mountains break up the simple pattern.**

HOLIDAY PLANNER
If you were planning your holiday just on the weather, where would you go? This map will help you to decide.

More photographs are on the Picture Gallery CD

WEATHER AROUND THE WORLD

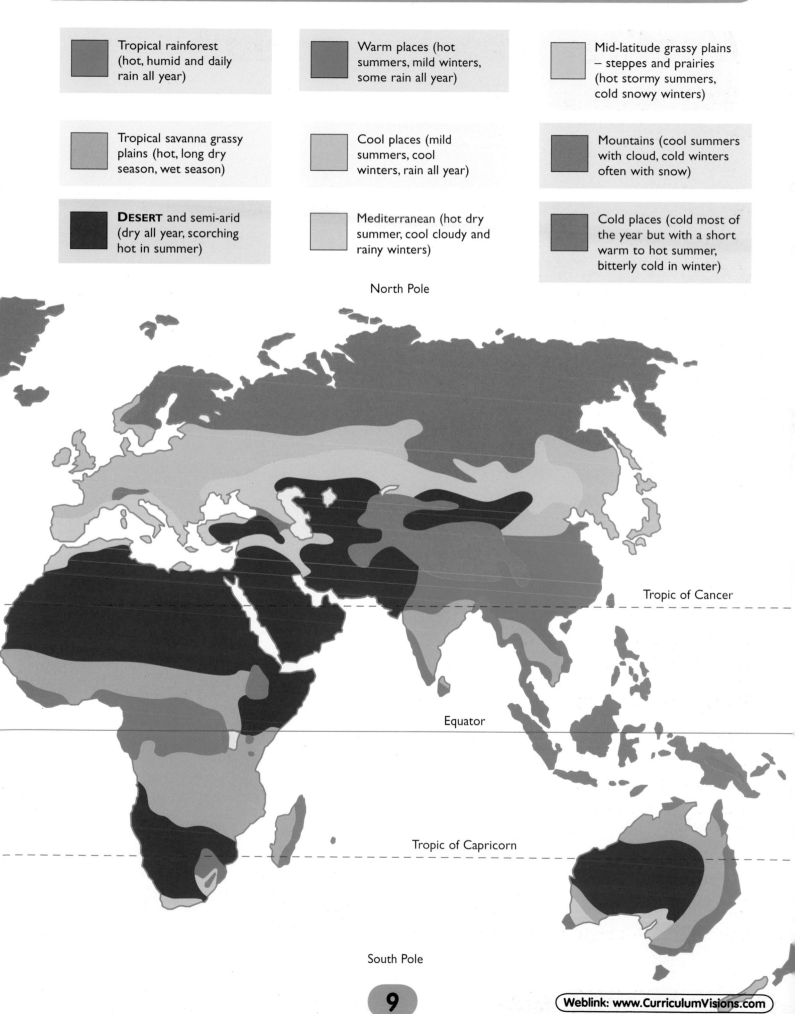

Tropical rainforest (hot, humid and daily rain all year)

Tropical savanna grassy plains (hot, long dry season, wet season)

DESERT and semi-arid (dry all year, scorching hot in summer)

Warm places (hot summers, mild winters, some rain all year)

Cool places (mild summers, cool winters, rain all year)

Mediterranean (hot dry summer, cool cloudy and rainy winters)

Mid-latitude grassy plains – steppes and prairies (hot stormy summers, cold snowy winters)

Mountains (cool summers with cloud, cold winters often with snow)

Cold places (cold most of the year but with a short warm to hot summer, bitterly cold in winter)

North Pole

Tropic of Cancer

Equator

Tropic of Capricorn

South Pole

What temperature means

Temperatures change through the day just as much as they change with the seasons.

It is striking how the weather changes from one part of the day to another, and from one day to the next. On these next few pages we will see why this happens.

Temperature

We measure warmth using a **THERMOMETER** (picture ①). The measure of warmth is called temperature. Thermometers are used to measure the temperature of the air. To get accurate readings thermometers are placed in the shade, often in special airy cabinets.

Thermometers are used to find out the average temperature each day of the year. We then use the temperature to say something about what the average weather is like at places all over the world.

Hot places

If you were going on holiday to a hot place, you would expect the temperature in the shade to be over 25°C whichever month you went there. Egypt is a hot place. If you stood in the sunshine in such places you might find it uncomfortably hot (picture ②). In hot places many people sit in the shade, perhaps under an umbrella on the beach (picture ③). Indoors they might use air

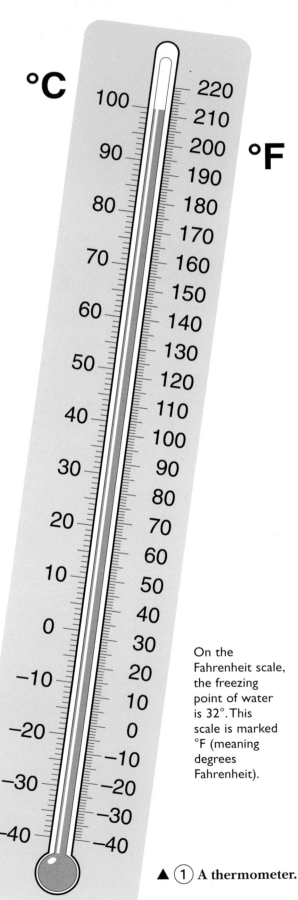

On the Celsius scale, 0° is the temperature at which pure water freezes. The Celsius scale is marked °C (meaning degrees Celsius).

On the Fahrenheit scale, the freezing point of water is 32°. This scale is marked °F (meaning degrees Fahrenheit).

▲ ① A thermometer.

▶ ② When people go to hot countries they should not go about in swimwear all day. Instead, they should wear clothes to cover their heads, arms and legs. Without this protection they might become overheated and fall ill (as well as receiving dangerous amounts of Sun, see page 12). These people are visiting the monuments of ancient Egypt. Look to see if they are at risk.

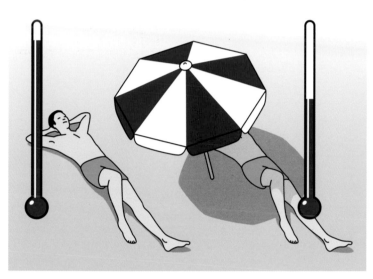

▲ ③ If you put a thermometer in direct sunlight, it will soak up the Sun's rays and become hot. This is also what happens to you when you sunbathe. If you go to a hot place, this would be uncomfortable as well as dangerous, which is why people use umbrellas on, for example, tropical beaches.

conditioning all year. In these kind of places you might go on holiday when they have their coolest part of the year.

Warm and cool places

If you went on holiday to a warm or a cool place, you would find that the temperature went above 25°C in some months, but in other months it would be 15°C or even lower. You might visit these kind of places during their summer, and perhaps late spring and early autumn. Sydney, Australia, is an example of a warm place. The UK is a cool place.

Cold places

If you went on holiday to a cold place you would find that the temperature went below freezing for many months of each year. In mountains you might visit them for skiing in winter or walking in their short summer.

What sunshine means for us

Sunshine is not the same as temperature. When you sunbathe there are important health considerations.

Close to the pole, low risk because the Sun's rays are more spread out by being at a low angle.

Close to equator, higher risk because the Sun's rays are concentrated by being overhead.

SUN

▲ (1) The overhead Sun is more dangerous than a low-angled Sun. The nearer you go to the equator for your holiday, the more the risk.

We all like sunny weather. Sunny weather warms the ground, and us, if we are out in it, making us feel good.

The Sun's rays, however, contain more than the **HEAT** rays we feel and the light rays we see. They also contain rays that we cannot see or feel. These include rays called ultraviolet or **UV RAYS**.

A small amount of UV rays are good for us because they make us healthier (our skin produces a vitamin called vitamin D when it is exposed to sunlight). But too much UV makes it more likely that we will develop skin cancer, which can be dangerous. Skin cancers are called melanomers.

Sunscreens

The stronger the sunshine, the more the risk. The risk is highest of all if we get sunburned regularly.

The Sun is stronger, the more overhead it is. So the middle of a sunny summer day is the time of greatest risk from sunny weather.

The Sun is never overhead in the UK, but when you get to the tropics it is always overhead at midday. So if you go on holiday to a country near the tropics, such as a Mediterranean country, or Florida, or Hawaii, the risk from UV is much greater than if you go on holiday in the UK. But even in the UK there is still a risk in high summer.

Sunscreens are lotions that contain substances that help to block the UV rays. Some lotions are stronger than others. You can tell how strong they are by looking at the UV factor on the bottle.

The UV weather rule

The brighter the Sun (the more overhead it is) the more UV rays soak into our skin. So the healthy balance is this: cover up during the peak hours of sunshine, work and play in the shade and if you are outside in the Sun use factor 15-plus sunscreen.

▼ ② People sunbathing on the beach in high summer in Bournemouth, UK. Lots of suntanned bodies, all hopefully protected by sunscreen lotions.

Weblink: www.CurriculumVisions.com

Places with hot and cold seasons

Temperatures in some parts of the world change with the seasons.

We all know there are four parts to any year: spring, summer, autumn and winter. These are the **SEASONS**. Our seasons, just like anyone else's living in the **MID-LATITUDES**, are controlled by how warm it is (pictures ① and ②).

You can often tell the seasons by studying the way plants behave (see postcard). From a weather point of view, this is better than dividing the year into four equal parts. Many plants start to grow in spring, get all of their leaves by summer, begin to lose them again in autumn, and are bare by winter. In some places this change is very dramatic.

The seasons lag behind the Sun

On page 8 we saw that the hottest time of day was later than when the Sun was highest in the sky.

ARCTIC

MID-LATITUDES (UK)

TROPICS

Places in this region have cool or warm summers and bitterly cold winters.

Places in this region have warm to hot summers and cool to cold winters.

Places in this region are always hot. They do not have hot and cold seasons.

▲ ① **The world's weather types, or climates, are divided up based on temperature.**

The same delay also happens in a year. The Sun is highest in the sky at the end of June, but the hottest time of the year is a month later.

The Sun is lowest in the sky, and shines for the shortest time, in December, yet the coldest time of the year is in January and February. This is because it takes time for the ground to warm up each spring. It also takes time for the ground to cool down each autumn.

A "Where in the world" postcard from (Curriculum Visions)

Dear Aunt Belinda,

Here we are in the Appalachian mountains of north east USA. It's truly wonderful in the autumn, or 'fall', as they call it.

The colours of these maple leaves show it well. In summer they were green, but as fall gets under way the cold air makes the leaves turn yellow then red.

Take care, Poppy

Late summer

Early autumn

Late autumn

▼ ② This is a yearly temperature chart for Oxford, England. The top part of the chart shows the Sun at noon. The lower part shows the average temperature for each month.

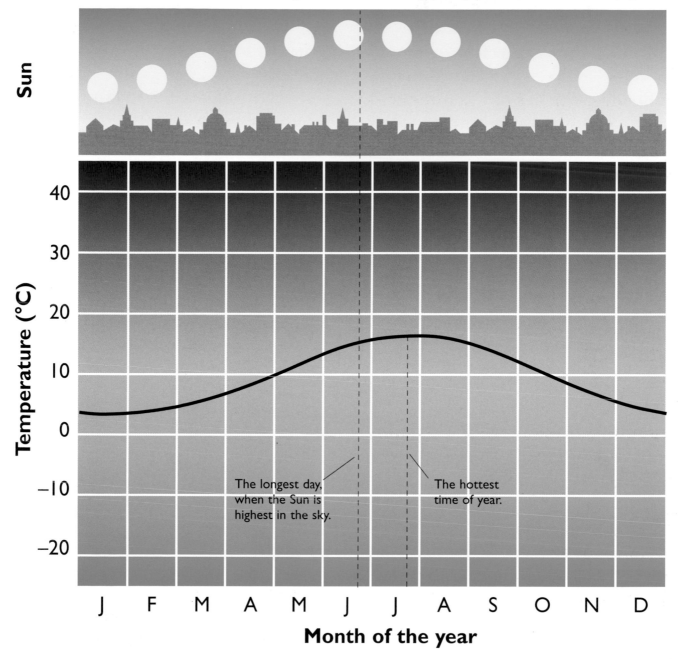

Sun

Temperature (°C)

40

30

20

10

0

−10

−20

The longest day, when the Sun is highest in the sky.

The hottest time of year.

J F M A M J J A S O N D

Month of the year

Winter: temperature at its minimum

Spring: temperature rising

Summer: temperature at maximum

Autumn: temperature falling

Weblink: www.CurriculumVisions.com

Rain, snow, dew and frost

Moisture is all around us as invisible vapour. But when air gets cold, the vapour changes to water or ice, not just in clouds, but on the ground as well.

We are all used to **RAIN**, but water in the air occurs in three forms: moisture (vapour), liquid (cloud droplets and rain) and solid (ice crystals in the shape of **SNOWFLAKES**) (picture ①). They all affect our weather.

Moisture

Water can change from liquid to invisible moisture. We call this **EVAPORATION**. When it changes back from vapour to liquid, we call it **CONDENSATION**.

Cloud and rain

Strangely, it is easy for liquid water to turn into moisture. It just needs warmth. It is much more difficult for moisture to turn into liquid water.

▼ ① **This diagram shows the many ways that condensation can occur. The movement of water from clouds to air, to ground, to clouds, is called the WATER CYCLE.**

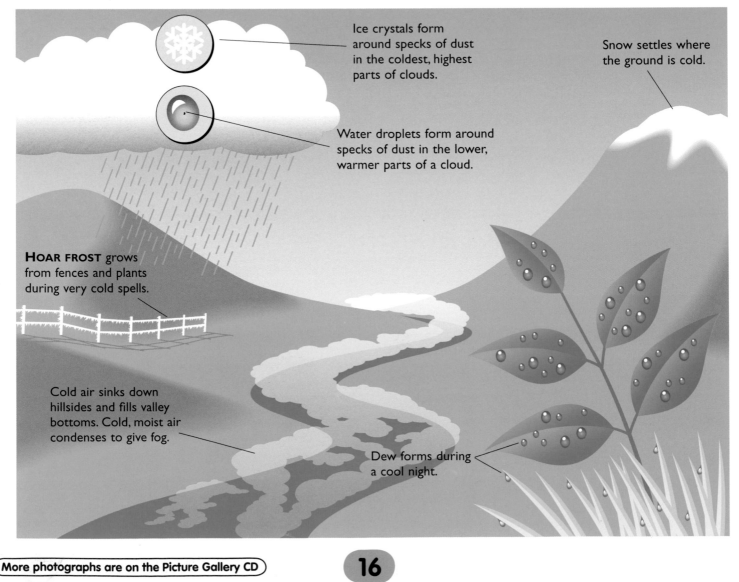

Ice crystals form around specks of dust in the coldest, highest parts of clouds.

Snow settles where the ground is cold.

Water droplets form around specks of dust in the lower, warmer parts of a cloud.

HOAR FROST grows from fences and plants during very cold spells.

Cold air sinks down hillsides and fills valley bottoms. Cold, moist air condenses to give fog.

Dew forms during a cool night.

▶ ② The amount of rain that falls depends on how much moisture is in the air. On hot days, large amounts of moisture are in the air, and when the moisture turns to droplets, torrential rain can be produced.

It needs a surface for the moisture to settle on to.

Specks of dust occur by the billion in the air. When moisture condenses on them, they make tiny beads of water called droplets. We see these as a **CLOUD**. When they fall from the cloud it rains (picture ②). We call the rain **DRIZZLE** if the drops are small.

▲ ③ When the air is very cold, vapour changes to ice and builds up as frost. You can see the individual ice crystals on this plant.

Dew and frost

When moisture settles out on the ground, we call it **DEW**. If the moisture then freezes, we call it **FROST** (picture ③).

Snow

Ice crystals form in cold clouds. Snowflakes are made of many tiny ice crystals clumped together. A combination of snow and wind produces a **BLIZZARD**.

Mist and fog

Cloud close to the ground gives mist or **FOG**.

Mist is when the air is not clear, but when you can see at least 1 km.

Fog is when the distance you can see is less than 1 km. Dense fog normally refers to when you can see less than 100 m.

By the way… The general name for all kinds of liquid and solid forms of water is PRECIPITATION.

Clouds

Clouds form when warm, moist air rises. The bubbly ones are called cumulus clouds. When the weather is hot, they follow a daily pattern.

A "Where in the world" postcard from (Curriculum Visions)

Dear Gill and Mike,

Howdy! This is what it's like in summer in Texas, USA. There are these cotton wool clouds dotted around the sky. Just the odd one is big enough to give rain, but it's so warm here the rain evaporates before it reaches the ground.

Yours, Kirk

There are two kinds of clouds: bubbly ones, which we call **CUMULUS**, and flat sheets of cloud, which we call **STRATUS** if they are thick and **CIRRUS** if they are wispy. You will find information on layer clouds on pages 30 and 31, here we look at bubbly clouds.

Bubbling – or cumulus – clouds are formed when air is warmed from below, for example, on a sunny day.

The clear sky allows the sunshine to warm the ground. Soon the ground shares its heat with the air, and bubbles of warmed air begin to rise. At first, the air is not very warm and only small bubbles form. But during the morning, as the ground becomes warmer and the air is heated more strongly, the bubbles get bigger and then great towering cumulus clouds may begin to cover the sky (picture ②).

▶ ① **The daily pattern of cumulus clouds. These diagrams show you how cumulus clouds grow in the morning, cover the sky and produce heavy showers during the afternoon, and then fade away by evening. This is a daily, or diurnal, pattern common in many parts of the world.**

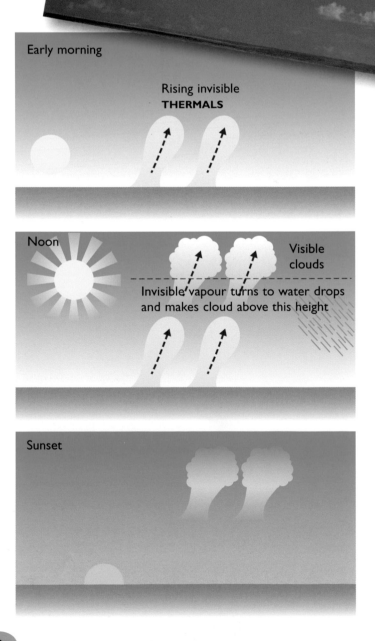

Early morning

Rising invisible **THERMALS**

Noon

Visible clouds

Invisible vapour turns to water drops and makes cloud above this height

Sunset

As the Sun goes down and the ground is heated less, so the clouds finally fade away (picture ①).

Rain clouds

Cumulus clouds do not all grow to be giants. Sometimes the air simply never gets hot enough, or there is not enough moisture to make droplets. These smaller, cumulus clouds are sometimes called 'cotton wool clouds'. Normally they tell of fine weather.

Only the bigger cumulus clouds produce rain. These are the ones with dark undersides. Giant cumulus clouds form only when the air is hot and humid. They can sometimes produce **THUNDER** and **LIGHTNING** (see pages 20 and 21).

▶ ② A bubbling cloud may have a 'life' as short as 20 minutes. Bigger clouds may last for a couple of hours. You don't notice them fade away because new bubbles are rising all the time to replace the old ones.

A "Where in the world" postcard from (Curriculum Visions)

Dear Aunt Ethel,

This is a thundercloud near the Grand Canyon in Arizona, USA. The park ranger was telling us that you get lots of these in summer when the hot ground makes the air rise and turn into droplets. When the droplets clump together they make rain. You can see rain is pouring out of the bottom of this dark cloud. These clouds are called cumulonimbus clouds, which means 'rain-bearing' cumulus. It sure did rain!

Best, Kathy

Thunder and lightning

Thunderclouds produce some of the most spectacular displays to be seen in the sky.

Giant cumulus clouds are the tallest clouds in the sky. They have fearsome **WINDS** within them that can cause thunder and lightning, as well as tornadoes (see page 24).

Thunderclouds form most often after a day of hot, muggy weather. Hot moist air contains the huge amount of energy needed to produce thunder and lightning.

How lightning is produced

LIGHTNING is a natural spark of static electricity (picture ①).

This flat spreading region of a cloud is called an anvil. It tells you that the cloud has reached the highest levels in the sky.

▼ ① This diagram shows a side view through a thundercloud.

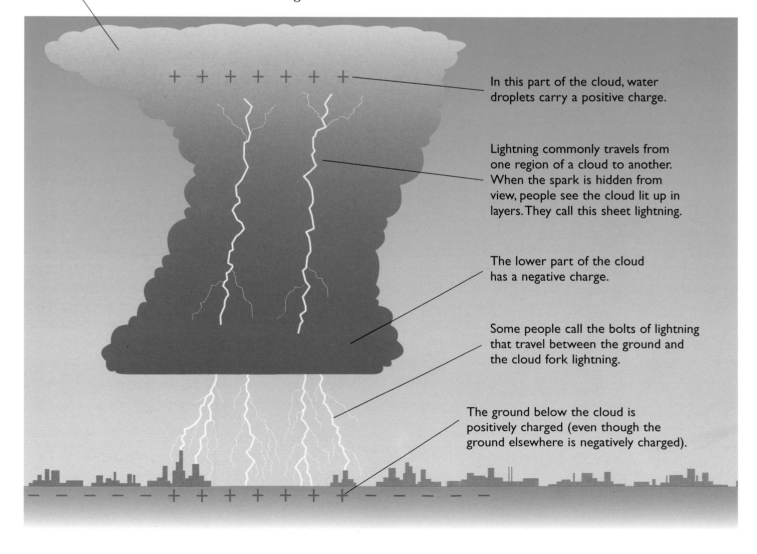

In this part of the cloud, water droplets carry a positive charge.

Lightning commonly travels from one region of a cloud to another. When the spark is hidden from view, people see the cloud lit up in layers. They call this sheet lightning.

The lower part of the cloud has a negative charge.

Some people call the bolts of lightning that travel between the ground and the cloud fork lightning.

The ground below the cloud is positively charged (even though the ground elsewhere is negatively charged).

Dear Jim,

We are sending this postcard from Florida, USA, one of the world's best places for seeing lightning. This spectacular picture shows many 'bolts' of lightning travelling between the base of the cloud and the ground.

Lightning is also attracted to upright objects such as trees, telegraph poles or tall buildings.

George and Annabel

Lightning is produced in a thundercloud because there the air is moving up and down very fast. The water droplets are swirled about and they brush against each other to make static electricity on the surfaces of all of the drops.

Opposite charges are needed for a spark. Lightning sometimes jumps from the bottom of the cloud to the ground (see postcard), or from the bottom of the cloud to the cloud top.

Thunder

As the spark jumps, it heats the air around it. The air expands so fast that it sets up shock waves in the air.

Static electricity

This sort of electricity is produced when one object brushes quickly against another. You can make sparks jump from your clothing by rubbing a plastic comb against your clothes very quickly, and then holding the comb a little way from your hand.

The shock waves are heard as **THUNDER**. To find out how far a cloud is from you, count the time in seconds from seeing the lightning to hearing the rumble of thunder. This number is the same as the distance to the cloud in miles.

Weblink: www.CurriculumVisions.com

Places with rainy seasons

In many tropical countries it is warm all the year, but rain falls only in certain months. As a result, many tropical places call their seasons by the amount of rain that falls.

Whereas people in the mid-latitudes describe their seasons by temperature changes (summer, autumn, winter and spring), there is little change of temperature in the **TROPICS**, and so the people who live there cannot use this way of talking about seasons.

▼ ①　This is the rainfall chart for Calcutta, India, a city famous for its MONSOON season of torrential rain. You should always look at a rainfall chart from a distance first. This way you can look at the shape. In this chart you will see that some columns are much taller than others. The tall columns show the rainy season. Some of the columns are very short; this is the dry season.

▲ ②　During the wet season the streets of Calcutta are almost permanently wet, and flooding is common. (Notice that many people are wearing shorts, because it is warm throughout the year in the tropics.)

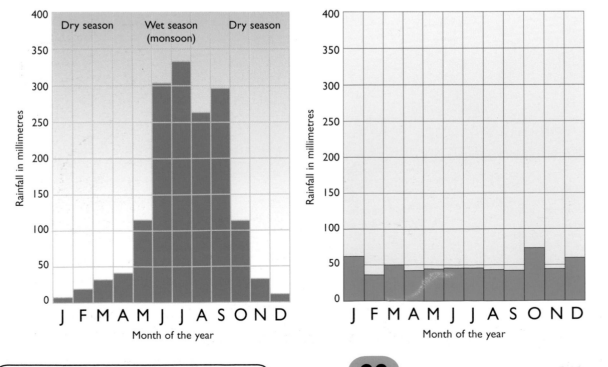

◄ Here is the pattern of rainfall in London so you can see how different Calcutta's rainfall is to ours.

Left chart:
Rainfall in millimetres — Month of the year
Dry season | Wet season (monsoon) | Dry season
J F M A M J J A S O N D

Right chart:
Rainfall in millimetres — Month of the year
J F M A M J J A S O N D

However, in many tropical places enormous amounts of rain fall at certain times of the year, while at other times there is no rain at all. As a result, many people in the tropics describe their seasons by rainfall, calling them **WET AND DRY SEASONS**.

You can see how seasons work in the tropics by looking at tropical Asia. The chart shows the rainfall in Calcutta, India (picture ①). You can see that, between June and September, a very large amount of rain falls. This is the rainy season. By October, very little rain falls, and the Sun shines almost every day for many months. This is the dry season. Pictures ② to ④ and the postcards on this page show you what the weather is like in tropical Asia.

A "Where in the world" postcard from Curriculum Visions

Dear Juliet,

This is a picture of the emerald-green paddy fields in Bali, Indonesia. It's sunny today, but the guide tells us the wet season that has just finished provides the water that is needed for rice to grow in paddy fields.

Yours, Kevin

▲ ③ Crops ripen after the rainy season and are harvested. The grass stops growing, making it difficult to feed animals. See how bare the ground is in the background. This is India in the dry season.

A "Where in the world" postcard from Curriculum Visions

Dear Joe,

I took this picture of myself during a monsoon rainstorm in Delhi, India, during July. You wouldn't believe how hard it rains during the monsoon. Just see how it is running over the ground. The rain falls in such large drops, it really hurts!

Dave

▲ ④ Without rain, the forests become parched and widespread forest fires are common. This is Thailand in the dry season.

Tornadoes

The world's fiercest winds occur in tornadoes. Although they last for just a few minutes, they can destroy houses and even lift cars and trains into the air.

Usually winds do not have a large influence on what we do. Winds are really only important when they become very strong and give **GALES** or worse (see page 45). The most severe windy conditions happen with tornadoes and hurricanes (page 26).

A **TORNADO** comes from the Spanish 'tronada', or **THUNDERSTORM**. Tornadoes are tightly spinning, funnel-shaped clouds that appear to hang from the bottom of a thundercloud (picture ①).

The winds in the centre of the funnel are the fastest in the world, some reaching 800 km/hr. They quickly pass over the ground, but the destruction they can cause in just a few minutes' passage can be tremendous (picture ②).

The size of a tornado

Tornadoes are produced as air is sucked very quickly into the bottom of a thunderstorm. They can form over land or water (where they are called **WATERSPOUTS**).

▶ ① These are the main features of a tornado.

The air spins violently in the funnel, which is why tornadoes are also given the nickname '**TWISTER**'.

Air flows into the bottom of the funnel very quickly, sucking up buildings, trees, locomotives, cars and anything else that is in its path.

Strong wind blows ahead of the tornado.

Funnel cloud writhes about, connecting the ground to the bottom of the thundercloud.

Intense rain falls from a tornado-bearing thunderstorm; thunder and lightning are also common.

▲ ② This tornado is clearly picking up enormous amounts of soil from the land, causing the funnel to turn black. The telegraph poles give the scale.

▼ The scale of severity of tornadoes.

Scale	Wind speed	Expected damage
F-0	70–109 km/hr	Slight damage
F-1	110–179 km/hr	Moderate damage
F-2	180–249 km/hr	Considerable damage
F-3	250–329 km/hr	Severe damage
F-4	330–414 km/hr	Devastating damage
F-5	over 415 km/hr	Incredible damage

▲ ③ Here you can see the close relationship between a tornado and a thunderstorm. Notice the lightning behind the tornado funnel.

Tornadoes may be just a few tens of metres across where they touch the ground; the biggest are only some hundreds of metres across (picture ③). They may last for less than an hour, and may travel just a few tens of kilometres.

Inside a tornado the air is very 'thin' (it is an area of very low pressure). Many buildings that have been tightly shuttered for protection often explode as a tornado passes because the air pressure inside the building remains much greater than that on the outside.

Tornadoes are very much smaller than hurricanes. You find tornadoes from the cool lands of the United Kingdom to the warmer areas of Australia, but they are by far the most common in the United States, which holds the world record at an average of 1,000 each year, most causing damage between May and July.

By the way... small tornado-like areas of spinning air are called WHIRLWINDS.

Weblink: www.CurriculumVisions.com

Hurricanes

Hurricanes (also called typhoons in Asia), are spirals of air from which torrential rain falls and the wind blows at more than 117 km/hr. Their winds can destroy houses and can also cause the sea to surge inland.

A "Where in the world" postcard from Curriculum Visions

Dear Auntie Liz,

We were so frightened the other day because we were here in Florida when a giant hurricane came drifting in from the sea. We were all evacuated inland and this picture shows what our beachside hotel looked like when we returned. So many homes were wrecked.

Gill

▲ ① This is a hurricane seen from space. Compare it with the cross-section on the opposite page.

HURRICANES are named after the West Indian word 'hurrican', meaning big wind. In the Western Pacific they are called typhoons (from the Chinese 'taifun', which means great wind).

Hurricane-force winds can uproot trees, demolish houses and leave a trail of death and destruction. Some of these winds may travel at the speed of a bullet – and do far more damage.

What is a hurricane?

Hurricanes are vast, swirling masses of cloud that mainly (but not always) move within and near the tropics (picture ①). They may travel many thousands of kilometres and they may last for weeks.

Hurricanes form only over hot oceans. Florida and the Caribbean islands are places which experience a hurricane season from late August to November. This is definitely not the most popular time to visit these places on holiday!

More photographs are on the Picture Gallery CD

▼ ② This is a cross-section of a hurricane. Notice that the clouds are caught in the spiralling winds. The eye is in the centre. The fiercest winds occur at the edge of the eye, a place called the eye-wall.

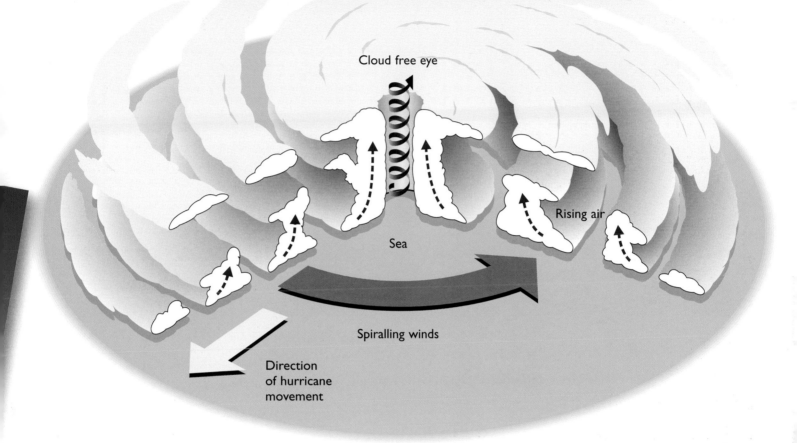

Cloud free eye

Rising air

Sea

Spiralling winds

Direction of hurricane movement

The hot ocean waters of late summer send heat and enormous amounts of moisture directly to the air. The hot, moist air then rises quickly. Then the moisture starts to turn back into water droplets, producing huge walls of cloud, releasing torrential rain and giving out vast amounts of heat energy (picture ②). The heat fuels the rising air.

The air soon begins to spin around a calm, often clear and sunny centre, called the **EYE**.

What happens inside a hurricane?

Think of a hurricane as a spinning top. The top spins furiously and wobbles in a curving path. The winds inside the hurricane may be going at over 117 km/hr. The hurricane itself, however, drifts from one place to another at a leisurely 12 km/hr.

Because a hurricane may be over 800 km across, the winds from a hurricane can batter an area for two days, with the most severe and damaging winds lasting for about 12 hours.

Settled weather

Settled weather occurs when air is still. In summer this gives hot sunny days, but in winter it gives cold weather and sometimes fog.

Have you ever noticed that sometimes the weather is very 'settled', while at other times it is very changeable? These changes give many of us the variety in our weather and it is the weather forecaster's job to foresee the patterns ahead. To do this, the forecaster needs to use two key words – **HIGH PRESSURE**, or **ANTICYCLONE**, and **LOW PRESSURE**, or **DEPRESSION**. In general, high pressure means settled, dry weather, and low pressure means changeable, rainy weather. The causes of settled weather can be seen here; you will find the causes of changeable weather on page 30.

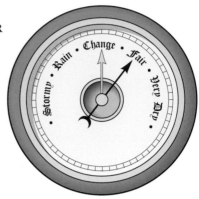

▶ ② A BAROMETER measures the pressure of the air. When the needle points to 'fair' or moves to the right, this tells of a high pressure.

Signs of settled weather

The telltale signs of settled weather are shown on a weather forecaster's map by the word **HIGH** (picture ①).

You can spot a high pressure even without a weather map. In summer, settled weather gives bright, sunny days with no more than small 'fair weather' cumulus clouds scattered across the sky (picture ③). Winter skies may also be fine and clear with pink and purple sunsets (see postcard). **FOG** is common overnight.

HAZE is another sign of settled weather. Haze occurs as the air fills with dust and prevents you from seeing long distances.

▲ ① This is what settled weather looks like on TV and on newspaper weather maps. Notice the word **HIGH**. The rings (called ISOBARS) give an idea of how windy it is: few rings – as here – are a sign of light winds. There are no WEATHER FRONTS in a high.

By the way… A high pressure occurs when air is settling down over a region, pressing down on the ground and squashing the air together, so increasing the AIR PRESSURE. This is what the barometer measures (picture ②).

The settling air stops most warm air bubbles rising. As a result there is often no cloud at all, even though the ground may be scorching hot.

▲ ③ In settled weather the sky may be clear, or small cumulus clouds may form. They do not grow, and so no rain can fall. This is why they are called 'fair-weather cumulus' clouds.

A "Where in the world" postcard from (Curriculum Visions)

Dear Kevin,

We are staying in Whitby in North Yorkshire. The weather has been very settled and sunny. This picture shows you the amazing sunset over the harbour. The red sunset means it will be fine again tomorrow, too.

Yours, Brenda

Changeable weather

Why does the weather change quickly in many parts of the world? The answer is usually connected with a WEATHER FRONT.

The telltale sign of changeable weather on a weather forecaster's map is the word **LOW** (picture ①). A barometer needle will also move to 'change' (picture ②).

A low is the opposite to a high. In a low, air is swirling upwards and lifting off of the ground (picture ③). This makes it easy for clouds to form even when there is no Sun to warm the ground.

Changeable sky

Unlike settled weather, the changeable sky is filled with cloud, usually sheets of layer cloud (picture ④).

◄ ① BAROMETER points to 'change', or moves to the left.

▼ ② This is what changeable weather looks like on weather maps: there are lots of rings (ISOBARS) that tell of windier weather and the word **LOW** in the centre. The fronts are marked by red and blue lines. This is where it is most likely to rain. The WARM FRONT is shown by a red line and the COLD FRONT is shown by a blue line.

▼ ③ This is a satellite picture of the map. You can clearly see the great swirl of cloud.

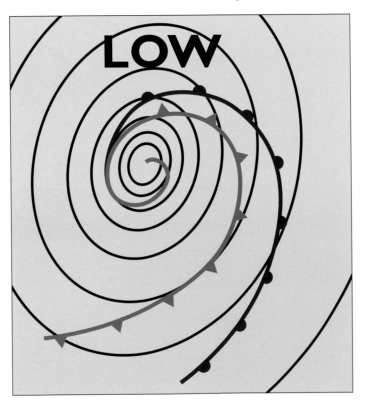

Forecasters use the word **FRONT** to show places where the main sheets of cloud form. The first sign of a front is a thin sheet of cloud high in the sky. This is cirrus cloud (picture ⑤).

Over the next few hours, the clouds will be lower, thicker and darker. These thick layers of cloud are called **STRATUS CLOUDS**. People call this an **OVERCAST SKY**.

Rain does not always fall, but all fronts are marked by overcast skies. Fronts mainly occur in pairs. When the sky brightens and the cloud breaks up, you know that the fronts have passed.

▼ ④ When a front is overhead, this is what you see. There are many layers of cloud above you. Together, they keep out most of the sunlight, and this is why they look dark.

▼ ⑤ This is what a side view through a low looks like. Notice thick heaps of cloud marking each front. Most lows have two fronts; the one on the right is called a warm front because warm air follows behind it; the one on the left is called a cold front because cold air follows behind it.

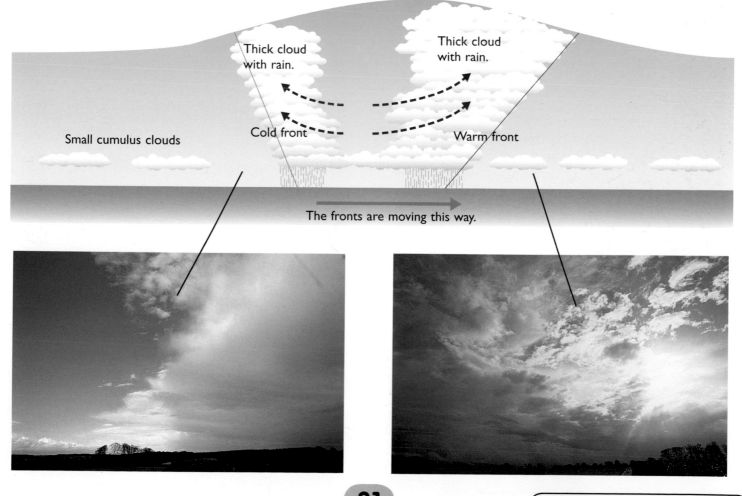

Thick cloud with rain.

Thick cloud with rain.

Small cumulus clouds

Cold front

Warm front

The fronts are moving this way.

Weblink: www.CurriculumVisions.com

Mountain weather

Air rises and sinks in valleys, giving mountains and valleys their own special weather.

When there is little wind, the weather can be affected by the local shape of the land, nearness to the sea or the presence of large cities. These all give rise to **LOCAL WEATHER**.

Shady and sunny valleys

In places with steep-sided valleys, one side of a valley can stay in shadow for much longer than the other side (picture ①).

The shady side of a valley stays much colder than the sunlit side. This is more important in winter, when the Sun is always low in the sky.

Crops, such as grapes, will ripen better on the sunny slopes than on the shady slopes.

People prefer to live on the warmer, sunny side rather than on the colder, shady side. This is one reason why villages and towns are often found only on the sunny sides of deep valleys.

▼ ① **This diagram shows how the rising Sun warms one side of a valley faster than the other. Villages in the Alps, for example, are placed to get the early morning Sun.**

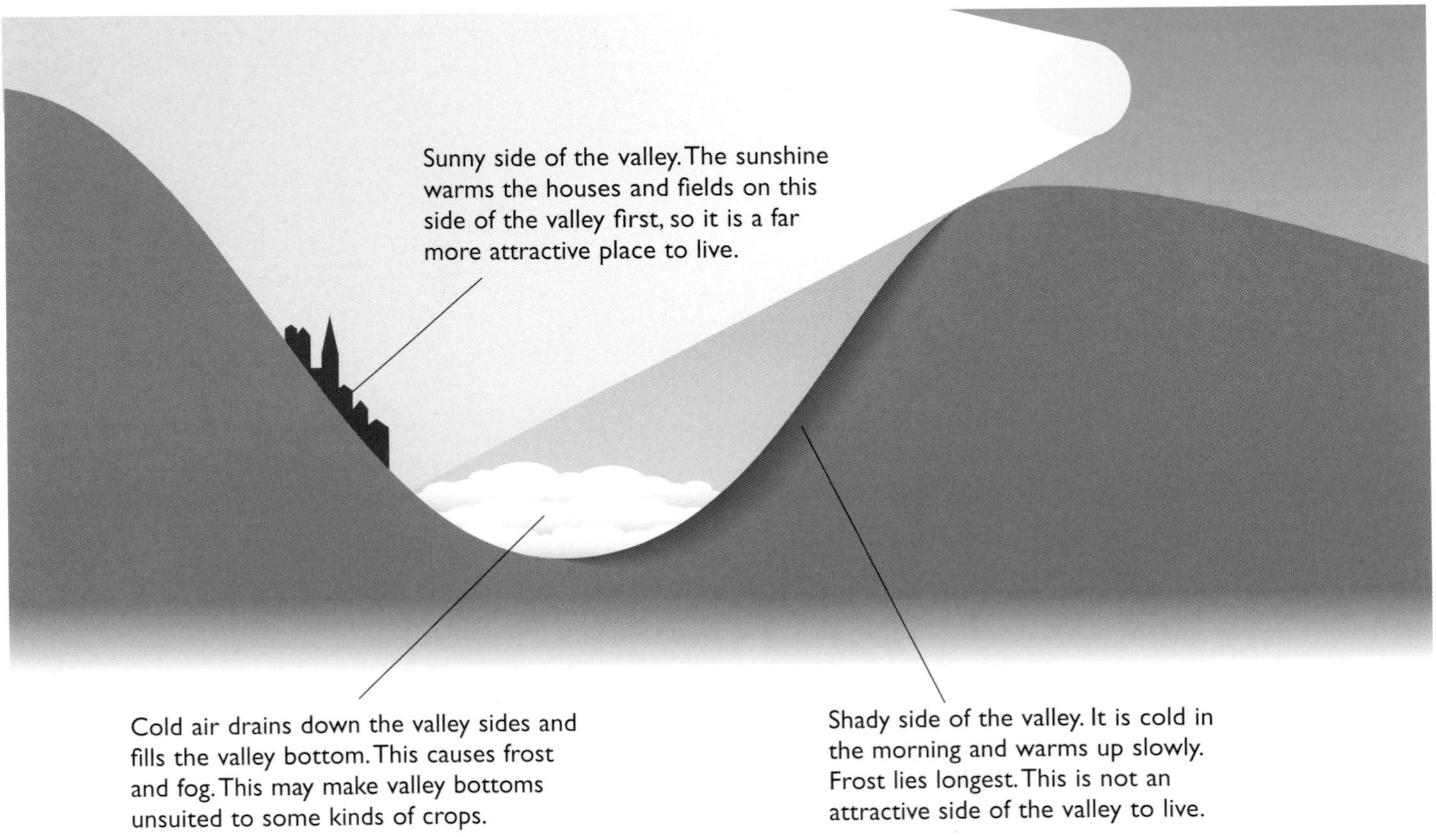

Sunny side of the valley. The sunshine warms the houses and fields on this side of the valley first, so it is a far more attractive place to live.

Cold air drains down the valley sides and fills the valley bottom. This causes frost and fog. This may make valley bottoms unsuited to some kinds of crops.

Shady side of the valley. It is cold in the morning and warms up slowly. Frost lies longest. This is not an attractive side of the valley to live.

Frost pockets

During the night the ground loses heat to the atmosphere, and the air close to the ground cools down.

Cold air is heavier than warm air and it rolls down hillsides, producing a night-time **BREEZE**.

When the cold air gets to the valley floor, it has nowhere else to go, so it builds up, often causing frost and fog, especially where there is plenty of moisture such as above rivers and lakes (see also picture ①, page 16).

Pollution traps

Valleys trap air, but they also trap pollution. This means that factories sited in valleys often make the air around them heavily polluted (picture ②).

Snowy passes

The higher you are, the colder it is. During winter many high valleys, especially mountain passes, receive snow instead of rain and the snow does not melt because the air is too cold (see postcard).

▼ ② Valleys in mountain regions are very sheltered places. See how the pollution from this factory is filling the valley bottom, rather than being blown away.

A "Where in the world" postcard from Curriculum Visions

Dear Jenny,

This is an amazing picture of our Alpine pass just being opened up in May. As you can see the snow is still really thick at these high altitudes. This pass has been blocked since November.

Yours, Bill

Seaside weather

The weather at the coast is often very different from that just a short distance inland. This is due to breezes blowing on and off the shore.

The sea changes temperature very slowly through the seasons. This is different to the land, which heats up and cools down quickly each day and also through the seasons.

▼ ① This picture shows cloud forming just inland of the coast of Florida. See how the coast remains sunny and clear. This pattern is the result of a sea breeze.

Sea breezes

The air over the sea is always moist. In summer the sea is cooler than the land. During the day the Sun heats the land and the air above it. This warmed air rises, pulling the cooler air in off the sea, and giving a cool **SEA BREEZE** (picture ①). This is why, when the land is hot, coasts are often the coolest, most comfortable places (picture ②).

▼ ② This diagram shows the way in which a sea breeze is produced. Notice that the breeze is set up because the land is warmed, causing the warmed air to rise. Cool air flows in from the sea to take the place of the rising warm air.

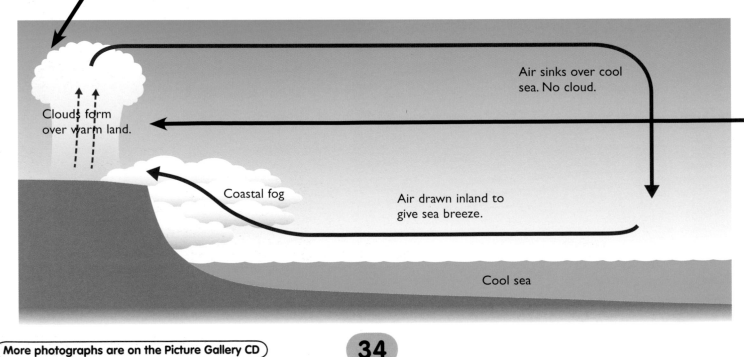

Air sinks over cool sea. No cloud.

Clouds form over warm land.

Coastal fog

Air drawn inland to give sea breeze.

Cool sea

A "Where in the world" postcard from Curriculum Visions

Dear Gran and Gramps,

This is what it looks like in Hawaii. There is a pleasant breeze on the beach, even on this scorching-hot, sunny day. It's a bit cloudy inland, as you can see, but that doesn't worry us here on the beach!

Best, Ned

Coast cloud and fog

Cloud often forms just inland of the coast even though the coast stays sunny (see postcard from Hawaii above). This happens when moist air crosses the coast and is forced to rise over the land.

By the time the air has cooled and produced cloud, it has travelled some distance inland, and so the coast stays clear.

In some places the cloud forms right against the coast, and this gives fog. San Francisco, USA, is a coastal city famous for its fog (see postcard below). Lima in Peru is another.

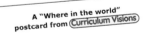

A "Where in the world" postcard from Curriculum Visions

Dear George,

This is a picture of San Francisco's Golden Gate Bridge. The city is out there in the fog.

For months of the year San Francisco gets covered in coastal fog every morning. It means that it is cool and you need to wear a jumper. Just the other side of the bridge the fog stops and there it is baking hot!

How weird!

Kate

City weather

Cities store and give out heat. The bigger the city and the more densely packed its streets, the more the weather differs from that in the surrounding countryside.

Have you noticed that it is often much warmer in a city than in the surrounding countryside? Because of this, trees come into leaf and leaves remain longest. The extra warmth can make cities more pleasant in winter, but more stifling in summer.

The extra warmth is caused by two things. Firstly, the buildings are heated in winter and this heat seeps out into the surrounding air. Secondly, the centre of a city has densely packed buildings that shelter the streets from strong winds, and trap warm air (picture ①).

Geographers call the warmer air in a city a **HEAT ISLAND**, because it is a small, warmer 'island' in a 'sea' of cooler countryside (picture ②). Early springs and late autumns are experienced in cities (picture ③).

▼ ② If you could see the air over a city, and if its colour showed how warm it is, this is what you might see! The air is warmer above the city centre, cooler in the suburbs and coolest in the open country. The symbols of thermometers show the heat island in side view and as a plan. You can find out how this works where you live by making a classroom project.

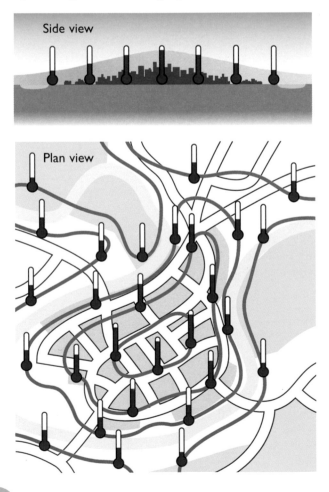

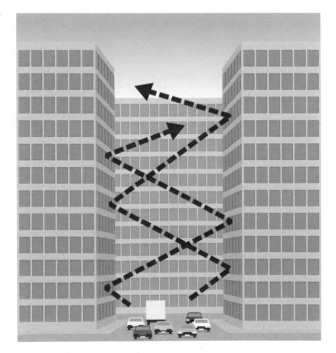

▲ ① Here you can see how heat bounces back and forth between buildings, keeping city streets warmer than elsewhere.

► ③ Spring comes sooner, and autumn lasts longer, in a city because the buildings keep it more sheltered and warmer. You notice this in the parks, where the flowers come out sooner and the trees stay in leaf longer. This is central Reading.

City pollution

Cities can also change the local weather because of the gases they send into the air. Car fumes contain many gases, as do fumes from power stations, factories, and so on.

Some of these gases combine with strong sunlight to make a kind of yellow–brown haze, known as SMOG (picture ④).

The gases can also be carried high into the air; here they mix with cloud droplets, forming acids. When rain falls from clouds like these, it is called ACID RAIN.

► ④ A yellow–brown pollution called smog hangs over some cities such as Los Angeles and Mexico City. It is especially bad in places which are built in basins surrounded by mountains, because here the air gets trapped and breezes are uncommon.

These pictures show Mexico City during a long, dry spell and after rain when the pollutants have just been washed out of the air. Notice that, when the air is polluted, you cannot even see the mountains in the distance.

Change: global warming and El Niño

► (1) Carbon dioxide traps some of the heat that would otherwise be lost to space. The more carbon dioxide there is in the air, the more heat is trapped. The extra heat stored in the air is often called the GREENHOUSE EFFECT.

▲ (2) This map shows which places seem to be getting hotter (pink) and which seem to be getting colder (blue) due to global warming. What is happening where you live?

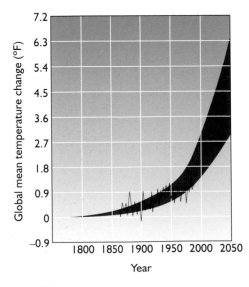

▲ (3) This graph shows how the Earth's temperature has changed over the last two centuries. The red band shows what might happen in the future.

Two weather events affect everyone in the world: global warming and El Niño.

Global warming

All of the HEAT that we receive from the Sun is gradually lost back to space. In this way the Earth doesn't naturally get hotter or colder.

What change means

Over the past centuries, burning coal and oil, or burning up forests, have added to the amount of carbon dioxide gas in the air. Carbon dioxide can trap heat (picture (1)). As a result the temperature of the air has been rising in many places (picture (2)). This is called GLOBAL WARMING.

The warming has already caused ice sheets to begin to melt in the Arctic and Antarctic. The water has caused sea levels to rise up to 25 cm, and further rises are sure to happen. This will cause low-lying coastal areas to flood in the near future.

Diseases that occur today only in the tropics may become more widespread. Some places will get too hot and dry to grow crops, and there may not be enough drinking water.

The only way to make global warming less severe is to reduce the amount of carbon dioxide in the air, which means burning less fuel (picture (3)). We can act now, while the problem appears small, to save the world's people from disastrous weather changes in the future.

El Niño

Every five or six years **DROUGHT** sometimes comes to regions that otherwise had plentiful rain, the **MONSOON** fails, and elsewhere floods are far more serious than normal.

These disaster-prone years are called **EL NIÑO** years, after the Spanish name for the Christ Child, since disasters begin to happen around Christmas time.

The disasters are caused by changes in the Pacific Ocean. Normally winds blow hot Pacific waters from east to west (from Peru to Indonesia). The peoples of the West Pacific, those in northern Australia and Southeast Asia, rely on the hot surface water as the source of moisture for their monsoon.

In an El Niño year the winds die down, so the water slowly spreads back eastwards (picture ④). In the West Pacific the ocean becomes cooler, less moisture evaporates, and the monsoons release less rain – they 'fail'. At the same time, the **DESERT** lands of North and South America experience a monsoon and become drenched in torrential rainfall.

These changes in the Pacific are so large that they push many of the world's weather systems out of position, leading to a whole chain of worldwide disasters (pictures ⑤ and ⑥).

▼ ④ This red area shows the places where the Pacific Ocean changes. It is a long band off the coast of Peru. A huge amount of water is involved, covering an area of surface water the size of Europe.

▼ ⑤ This map shows the places in the world most affected by El Niño. Notice how Eastern Australia and Southeast Asia suffer drought (red), as do India and Southeast Africa, while Northeast Africa, Peru and California suffer torrential rainstorms (green).

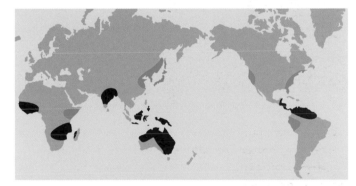

▼ ⑥ Disastrous fires are an important El Niño effect. In recent years widespread fires have raged in El Niño drought areas, for example Australia and Indonesia.

Measuring temperature changes

Wherever you are in the world it is warmest by day and coolest by night. This is because we owe our warmth to the heating power of the Sun.

Have you noticed that the warmest part of the day is in the early afternoon, not at midday when the Sun is highest? This is because it takes time for the air to warm up each day, just as it takes time for the air to cool down each night.

This is the daily pattern everywhere in the world (picture ②). Wherever you are, it is coolest just after dawn and hottest in the early afternoon.

The two temperatures that most easily sum up the whole day are the hottest (**MAXIMUM**) and coldest (**MINIMUM**).

An easy way to measure the maximum and minimum temperatures in a day is to use a special maximum–minimum thermometer (picture ①).

Making a chart of how temperature changes

If you were to measure the temperature throughout the day, you could plot the results as a graph like the ones here (pictures ③ and ④).

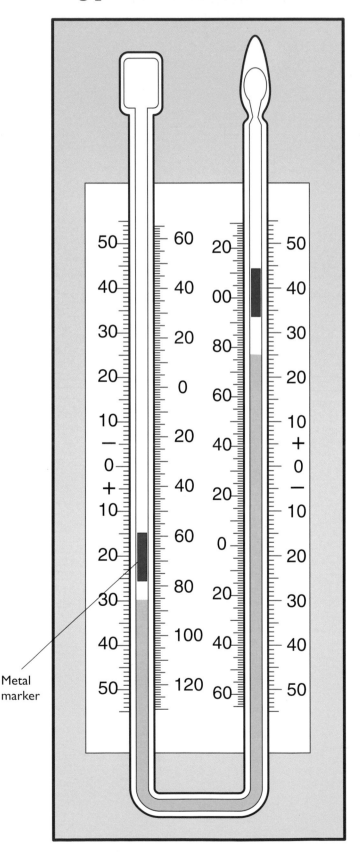

Metal marker

▶ ① This maximum–minimum thermometer will tell you the highest and lowest temperatures of the day.

The tube contains two small metal markers that are pushed by the mercury as it moves around the U-shaped tube. The markers are held in their farthest positions by a magnet behind the scale.

Sun

 ② At dawn each day the Sun rises. It is at its highest at noon. It then sinks again, disappearing at sunset. This pattern is shown here.

Temperature

Time

◀ ③ How to make a graph of temperature changes throughout the day.

If we sketched a thermometer every two hours during the day and then placed the sketches side by side, we would get this picture. It shows directly how temperature changes.

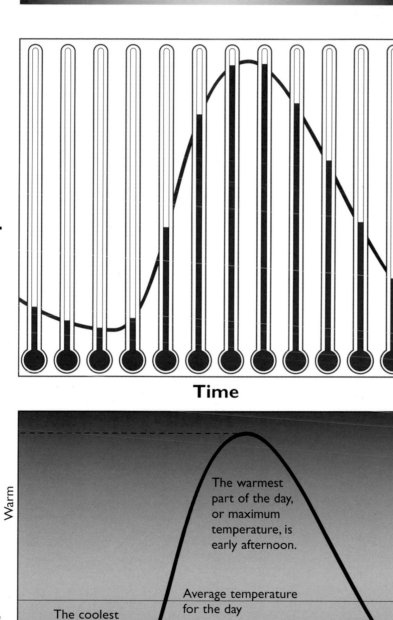

Temperature

Warm

Cool

The warmest part of the day, or maximum temperature, is early afternoon.

Average temperature for the day

The coolest part of the day, or minimum temperature, is around dawn.

Midnight   Midday   Midnight

Time

◀ ④ This graph shows the temperature changes during a day.

Measuring and charting rainfall

Rain gives the moisture that allows plants to grow. Too much rain makes flooding likely; too little rain gives droughts. Measuring rain tells us what to expect.

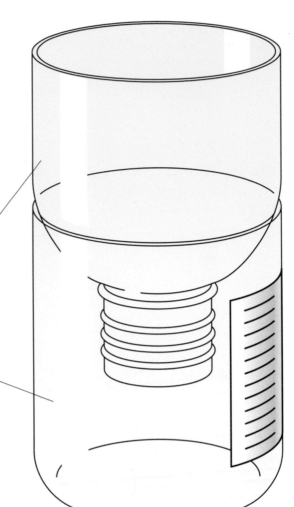

Plastic bottle cut in two, with top upside-down in the base. The top acts as a funnel.

The scale is stuck on the side.

We might think that cold days are unpleasant, but days without rain can spell disaster for crops and our food. This is why it is important to know how much rainfall to expect and how variable it is likely to be.

Measuring rain

Rainfall is one of the most easily measured parts of the weather. This is how you can do it as a project. Rain is measured using a **RAINGAUGE** (picture ①).

Rainfall is most commonly measured in millimetres. This small unit is used because, in most places, only small amounts of rain fall each day.

▲ ① To make a simple raingauge, cut off the bottom of a soft-drinks bottle. Turn the top upside-down and use it as a funnel. Place the raingauge inside a flower pot large enough to leave a wide gap all around the raingauge. Bury the flower pot in the ground so that the rim of the raingauge is level with the ground.

To make a scale, pour known amounts of water into the raingauge from a scientific measuring jar and mark the different levels on the side of the gauge.

Making a rainfall chart

Rainfall is normally measured just once a day, usually at 9 am. You can make a daily rainfall chart from your measurements of rainfall, or you can add up each day's rainfall

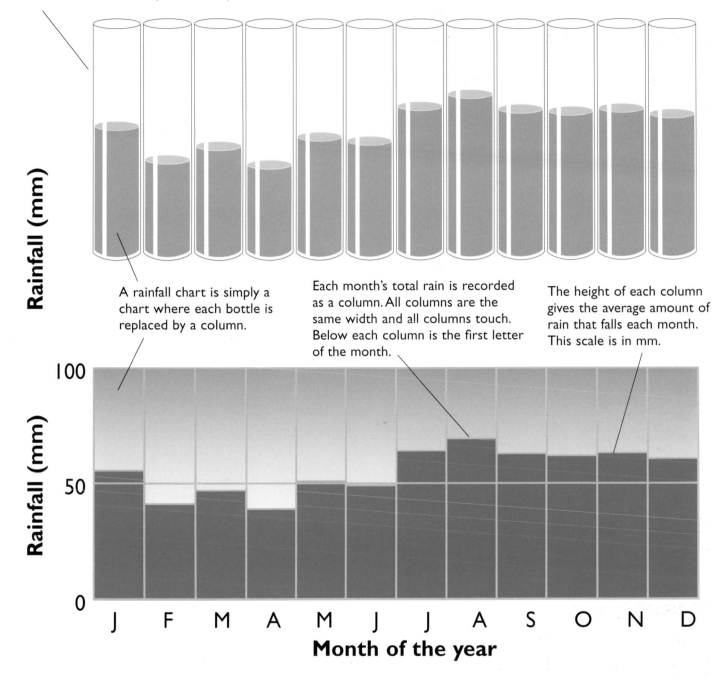

This is what the water collected in raingauge bottles for each month of the year would look like if the 12 bottles were placed side by side.

Rainfall (mm)

A rainfall chart is simply a chart where each bottle is replaced by a column.

Each month's total rain is recorded as a column. All columns are the same width and all columns touch. Below each column is the first letter of the month.

The height of each column gives the average amount of rain that falls each month. This scale is in mm.

Rainfall (mm)

100

50

0

J F M A M J J A S O N D

Month of the year

to give a monthly total and draw a chart for the year. Most rainfall charts are yearly charts.

The best way to plot rainfall is to use a column chart. Picture ② shows what a rainfall chart might look like for one year.

▲ ② This is what a yearly rainfall chart looks like for Edinburgh, Scotland. The chart shows the average rainfall for each month. Notice that there is not much difference between months, although spring is slightly drier than other times of the year.

By the way… Snow depth is measured with a ruler pushed through the snow to the ground. About 12 cm of freshly fallen snow contains the same water as 1 cm of rainfall.

Measuring the wind

Breezes, winds, gales and hurricanes are all forms of air on the move.

The air all around us is made of gases. We don't see them, but when they move we can feel them as **WINDS**.

Measuring the wind

Wind has both strength and direction. The simplest way to measure the wind direction is with a **WIND VANE** (picture ①).

A **WIND SOCK** is a simple instrument that gives a rough idea of both wind speed and direction (picture ②).

A "Where in the world" postcard from Curriculum Visions

Dear Liz,

Here we are in late spring near Malaga in the Costa del Sol in Spain, and what a surprise. There is a gale blowing, which I am told happens every year at this time.

I know it's hot and sunny in the summer, but it's not like that just at the moment!

Best, Fred.

An instrument called an **ANEMOMETER** is used to measure wind speed accurately (picture ①).

▼ ① A wind vane and anemometer are often mounted together as part of an electronic weather centre. Leads from each instrument go to a computer that shows the wind speed and direction.

The blade acts as a wind vane. The smallest end of the blade faces the wind.

These cups catch the wind and spin the shaft around.

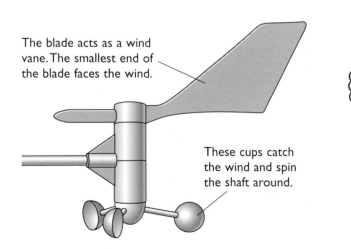

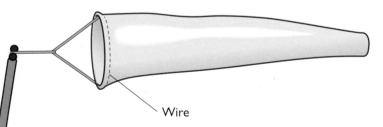

Wire

▲ ② The strength of the wind can easily be seen using a wind sock. To make a wind sock like the one shown below, you need a tube of lightweight material, such as nylon, a piece of wire and a stick. Make a circle of wire to keep the end of the sock open and stitch the sock to the wire. Tie the sock to a stick using a loop of string, as in the picture. When the wind blows, the wind sock will fill with air and rise clear of the stick: the stronger the wind, the higher the end will rise. The foot end of the sock will point away from the wind.

WEATHER PROJECTS

A wind scale

Not everyone has an instrument for measuring wind speed. Many years ago a wind scale was developed for the Navy by Admiral Beaufort. The **BEAUFORT SCALE**, shown below, was named after him. Notice that it uses simple observations to give an idea of wind speed (picture ③).

Looking at trees and plants

Plants and trees can tell you what the wind is like, on average. Where strong winds commonly blow from the same direction (known as **PREVAILING WINDS**), plants turn away to protect themselves. Check this out on hilly land or by the seaside.

▼ ③ The Beaufort scale

0

Calm
Calm; smoke rises vertically.

1

Light air
Direction of wind shown by smoke drift, but not by wind vanes.

2

Light breeze
Wind felt on face; leaves rustle; ordinary vane moved by wind.

3

Gentle breeze
Leaves and small twigs in constant motion; wind extends light flag.

4

Moderate breeze
Raises dust and loose paper; small branches are moved.

5

Fresh breeze
Small trees in leaf begin to sway; crested wavelets form on inland waters.

6

Strong breeze
Large branches in motion; whistling heard in telegraph wires; umbrellas used with difficulty.

7

Near gale
Whole trees in motion; inconvenience felt when walking against the wind.

8

Gale
Breaks twigs off trees; generally impedes progress.

9

Strong gale
Slight structural damage occurs (chimney pots and slates removed).

10

Storm
Seldom experienced inland; trees uprooted; considerable structural damage occurs.

11

Violent storm
Very rarely experienced; accompanied by widespread damage.

12

Hurricane
Severe damage.

Weblink: www.CurriculumVisions.com

Glossary

ACID RAIN Rain that has been polluted with acid gases.

AIR PRESSURE The weight of the atmosphere caused by gravity pulling gas molecules towards the centre of the Earth. A region of high pressure is formed where air currents cause dense air to sink over a region of the Earth; in a region of low pressure air rises, and is less dense.

ANEMOMETER An instrument for measuring wind speed.

ANTICYCLONE A high pressure area in the lower atmosphere. An anticyclone contains sinking air, and cloud is uncommon.

BAROMETER An instrument for measuring the pressure of the atmosphere.

BEAUFORT SCALE A scale for measuring wind speed in units from force 0 (calm) to force 12 (hurricane force).

BLIZZARD A snowstorm accompanied by driving winds such that the snow moves almost horizontally.

BREEZE A gentle wind. On the Beaufort scale a breeze is regarded as a flow of air less than 27 knots. *See also:* sea breeze.

CIRRUS CLOUD Thin veil-like or wisp-like ice clouds that form in parts of the atmosphere where only ice crystals (snowflakes) can form.

CLIMATE The long-term, or average kind of weather, that might be expected at any location over a year.

CLOUD A large number of water droplets and/or ice crystals suspended in the atmosphere.

COLD FRONT The boundary between warm and cold air immediately behind an area of low pressure.

CONDENSATION The process where water vapour changes to liquid water on contact with a cold surface. A common form of condensation is dew.

CUMULUS CLOUD Individual clouds that form in a sky when warmed air rises. They are especially dramatic in the tropics and in the centres of mid-latitude continents during the hot summer season when they can bring downpours and create tornadoes.

DEPRESSION (Also called low pressure), a huge swirling mass of air in mid- and high-latitude regions of the Earth. A depression brings together cold moist air from polar regions and warm moist air from the tropics. See low pressure.

DESERT Regions of very low rainfall and extremely sparse vegetation. They cover about a sixth of the Earth's land surface. They fall into three groups: (i) hot deserts, (ii) cold deserts and (iii) rainshadow deserts.

DEW Moisture that settles on grass and other surfaces when air cools. The temperature at which dew forms is called the dew point.

DRIZZLE Light rain.

DROUGHT A long, unusual period without significant rainfall. Some parts of the world, particularly between latitudes 1 and 20 degrees, have a more variable rainfall pattern than others and so they can be said to be more drought-prone.

EL NIÑO A global change in the world's weather that occurs about every five or six years.

EVAPORATION The loss of water from a surface due to the drying effect of the air.

EYE The central calm region of a hurricane.

FOG Cloud that forms at ground level. Cold sea or land conditions cause the air to cool and some of the moisture in it condenses into tiny water droplets. The more water droplets that form, the thicker the fog. The thinnest form of fog is called mist.

FRONT Used by meteorologists to describe the boundary between two types of air in the atmosphere. Fronts are nearly always marked by a broad belt of cloud and rain.

FROST Occurs when moisture in the air freezes onto surfaces, producing a thin film of ice crystals. Freezing normally occurs when the temperature of the surface falls below 0°C.

GALE A strong wind: Force 8 (gale), force 9 (severe gale), force 10 (full gale or storm) on the Beaufort scale.

GLOBAL WARMING The gradual warming of the atmosphere due to the Greenhouse Effect.

GREENHOUSE EFFECT The gradual warming of the world's atmosphere due to the increase in the amount of carbon dioxide in the air.

HAZE Reduced visibility caused by the build-up of dust particles in the air.

HEAT The part of the Sun's energy that causes temperature to rise.

HEAT ISLAND The region around a city which remains up to several degrees warmer than the surrounding countryside, either on still summer nights or during calm spells in winter.

HIGH PRESSURE The build-up of air in a part of the atmosphere. It is often used as an alternative to anticyclone.

HOAR FROST A build-up of ice crystals on a surface during frosty weather.

HUMIDITY The relative moisture content of the air; more properly relative humidity.

HURRICANE A name for severe low pressure regions that develop in and near to the tropics.

ISOBAR A line drawn on a chart to represent places having the same atmospheric pressure. Isobars help to predict the strength of the wind because the closer the isobars lie, the stronger the wind will be.

LIGHTNING A natural spark between different layers of a cloud or between a cloud and the ground.

LOCAL WEATHER The particular regional effects that show up when the air is calm.

LOW PRESSURE A part of the atmosphere where air rises causing changeable weather. Another word used is depression.

MAXIMUM The highest value.

MID-LATITUDES The band of Earth between the tropics and the Arctic or Antarctic.

MINIMUM The lowest value.

MOISTURE See humidity.

MONSOON A rainy season which starts very abruptly. Countries that experience monsoons are all within, or close to the tropics. The monsoon is particularly associated with India.

OVERCAST SKY A sky that is covered with clouds, usually layer clouds.

PRECIPITATION A general term for all forms of water particles – rain, snow, sleet, dew, hail, etc.

PREVAILING WIND The most commonly occurring wind direction.

RAIN/RAINFALL Droplets of moisture that have become big enough to fall out of clouds. They are one form of precipitation.

RAINGAUGE An instrument for measuring rainfall.

SEA BREEZE A coastal wind set up by the heating effect of the land relative to the sea.

SEASON A period of the year which has a marked character (for example, summer is hot; a dry season has very little rain).

SMOG A combination of fog and smoke.

SNOWFLAKES Snow is made of small crystals of frozen water – ice crystals – high up in cold clouds. A snowflake is a group of ice crystals that have become heavy enough to fall from a cloud.

STORM The name for severe weather with heavy rain and strong winds. The most severe forms of storms are hurricanes, also called typhoons.

STRATUS CLOUD The word stratus means layer. Stratus clouds are layer clouds, usually in the mid and high altitudes. Stratus cloud at ground level is experienced as fog.

SUNSHINE For weather, this is the heat energy from the Sun.

THERMAL An upward-moving flow of warm air caused by ground heating. Cumulus clouds form as a result of thermals.

THERMOMETER An instrument for measuring temperature.

THUNDER The sound produced by a lightning flash.

THUNDERSTORM A storm that is localised to a single thundercloud. Thunder is associated with tall cumulonimbus clouds.

TORNADO Originally the Spanish word for thunderstorm, tornadoes are violently spinning funnels of air that follow the base of severe thunderstorm clouds.

TROPICS The region between the Tropics of Cancer and Capricorn.

TWISTER A common name for a tornado.

UV RAYS Short for ultraviolet radiation, a range of invisible Sun's rays that are important to good health in small amounts, but which may be harmful if the skin is overexposed.

WARM FRONT A sloping boundary between cold and warm air in a depression. A place where cloud and rain are most likely.

WATER CYCLE The way that moisture circulates as vapour, liquid and solid between land and air.

WATERSPOUT A tornado over water.

WEATHER The short-term nature of the atmosphere. People ask "What will the weather be like tomorrow?"

WEATHER FRONT The region where cool air meets warm air. A place of cloud and rain. See cold front and warm front.

WET AND DRY SEASONS The seasons that people experience in much of the tropics.

WHIRLWIND A violently spiralling column of air, similar to, but smaller than, a tornado. Whirlwinds have many regional names including 'dust devil' and 'willy willy'.

WIND The rapid movement of air.

WIND SOCK A conical instrument used to measure wind speed and direction.

WIND VANE A plate that swivels in a wind to show wind direction.

Index